Esther's Poems

Esther's Poems

Esther Franklin

Library of Congress Control Number: 2020901116
ISBN: Hardcover   978-1-7960-8417-7
                 Softcover   978-1-7960-8416-0
                 eBook   978-1-7960-8415-3

Print information available on the last page.

Rev. date: 02/17/2020

To order additional copies of this book, contact:
Xlibris
1-888-795-4274
www.Xlibris.com
Orders@Xlibris.com
794927

Contents

For and About YOUNG
GRANDCHILDREN

Memories Of Floral Avenue

New and Old Memories Blend Together
When Deaths and Holidays Bring Us Close

Joann's PASSING takes us back to the Wife
Who brought Changes into Moffet's Life
His Career With Standard Began to Boom
Success in Multiple Ways would Loom
Leaving Your Child With a Sister Wasn't New
Until you get the 3-Year-Old's Point of View
Esther Said Falling From Tree Might Be a Loss
Shauna said, "YOU'RE NOT MY BOSS!!"

THEN RISES the MEMORY OF 2-PLUS LARRY
Whose WANDER AWAY was Really SCARY
Back home with SHERIFF; Easy for Him to See
"HORSIES NOT AFRAID OF ME!"

To Ten-Year-Old

in
Spanish Dancer's Dress

You pose;
I gasp and yearn
(Eyes drop to heart
held by clutching hand)

FREEZE TIME!
Keep the child
In view.

Alas!
You've gazed in Carmen's mirror
Seen dancing diva
Clapped on by crowds

I must not pine
I must luxuriate, appreciate

Let tomorrow's camera reflect
Pull on future strings

Written for Natalie from Nana,
Valentine's, 2000

SPECIAL EVENTS

"Being Rich"

What does it mean "To be Rich"?
Does it mean having more money
Than you've ever had before?
Or Beautiful Flowers on your door?
Does it mean Dancing with a Son
Who makes the experience great fun?
Or being with his Precious Wife
Who is still the light of his life
Maybe it's having Canadian kids near
Close-Up Reminders--why they are dear
Perhaps John coming to Sac alone
Andrea with us only by phone
Just the SURPRISE of D&V here
What a JOY! That was so clear!
The Taylors took care of me sick
Their 3-day Plan went by too quick
I AM GRATEFUL FOR ALL THE ABOVE! I AM RICH!!!

Can It Be

Can this be the precious baby from whom we all waited?
That baby who wanted no relative to hold her –
excepting her mother>

Can this be the toddler who played in the Almanor Snow
- even though it was Easter?

Can this be the angel who danced in the Nutcracker
and planned a career in Ballet?

Then she was THE SUPER SWIMMER --
the Medal-Winning Champ

On the Captain of the Water Polo Team
at McClatchy High

Could that have been our Natalie-one of a Trio
Singing to the High School Graduation Crowd?

Her next focus was on Turtles down in Costa Rica --
Environmental Reasons, of course!

What did we miss while she concentrated so hard?
on Studies, while home was the Dorm?

Time races; the University is in Spain,
but Travelling too is part of the plan:

Holidays with Relatives in the Alps to snowboard,
then Easter with the Pope, plus Venice too

How many countries? Were there really ten?
And how did the African markets fit it?

Home to Chaos re financing the State U System
Another year? Plus tuition going up?
Not 5 years! Change; the Major to Spanish and
Work unbelievably hard!!

Can it be? She did it, and now
She's GRADUATE NATALIE with her B.A!

We all are very PROUD of you,
Miss GLOBAL CITIZEN

Still, truthfully, (maybe wistfully)
Nana asks, "CAN IT BE?"

From Nana --, Natalie's graduation from
          San Francisco State University,
          May 21, 2011

Celebrating Serena

OUR "WITH HONORS" PH. D. RECIPIENT

We knew the "horse girl", who showed us how to ride
"She'll be a vet someday," her folks would say with pride
(I had a son so much like that, I mused
Was it summer work which made him less enthused?)

It's SERENA now on whom we're CONCENTRATING
Her RECENT ACCOMPLISHMENTS we are celebrating!!

Was it the way your parents used their lives?
Inspiration guides the path on which one strives
We admired the way you changed your course – making
Nutrition Research
<u>Your cart</u> before the horse!

Your dad's with us here today
Of your honors he is proud
He's cheering in his quiet way
(He was never loud)
He loved the wedding too.

Now we're wond'ring, what's the next move?
Will helping Diabetes be your thing,
Or is there still another grove?

We're sure that SERVICE ranks high among the CHOICES
What'ere you (with Ryan) choose, please know
This room is filled with clapping voices!!!

Written with great love by "Great Aunt" Esther
for June 10, 2010

Celebration

Written for ONE WORLD Official Opening, August 2, 1994

You laughing ones
Here to nibble
At world's food
To drink the joy

Do you know
Of February fatigue?

Family Royalty

GREAT – GRANDMOTHER DELLA
BEGAN THIS RECOGNAITON WAY
"A NURSE WITH A DEGREE"
IS WHAT THEY WOULD SAY.
MUCH LATER EMPORIA STATE HAD
NOT HAD ONE 'TIL THEN
WHO TOOK 75 YEARS BEFORE
COMING TO COLLEGE AGAIN

NOW IN TWO-THOUSAND SIX-TEEN
WE HAVE FAMILY THEY CALL "QUEEN."
TO ADD TO THIS FUN THING
HER DATE THEY CALL "KING."
WE RAISE OUR GLASSES TO YOU!
EAT A BITE OF SPECIAL CAKE TOO!
FOR NOW" "HAVE JOY AND FUN
<u>CELEBRATE</u> WHAT YOU'VE BEGUN!"

Memories Wedding Present

Wedding Presents One Often Finds
Will be of Very Different Kinds
Some Will Have Been Purchased at Great Cost
<u>Others Will Bring Back Memories Almost Lost</u>
The First Related Name that You Will Hear
Will not be Familiar to Your Ear
"Great Grandma Della" is here to Make You Savor
MEMORIES THAT HAVE A RURAL FLAVOR
This was HER PITCHER, but Unlike Now
She Used It To Pour Milk Right From the Cow
We Drink Milk that has been taken to Town
Handled in Ways On Which We Could Frown
Who Has Touched the Boxes We Get From the Store?
Not Just the Clerk, But Many More!
So NANA Very Much Hopes You Will Soon Savor
MILK THAT HAS A RURAL MEMORY FLAVOR!

Written by NANA for TRISH & Nate – November 19, 2019

Prescription For "Better"

Honored are you shoes work focused on circles
Circles of small glass which helped others see
Now a circle of another kind closes 'round
To sing your praise (or click a fault or two.)

Many have raised high the toasting glass
Shared lights from memory's shining mirror
As Elder of this clan, I bring sage words
Insights, cautions about Senior Life

Soon you'll hear the simple words,
"Since you're not working now"
BEWARE!. That translates to
Long hours with no pay.

Anon--I rush too fast with warnings
'Ere the traveler's journey starts, questions
Must be asked --Profound queries, like
"What ya want outa life?"

'Tis I, the Questioner, who dons the magic coat
'Tis I who will control the blinding lights.
Who will peer into your eyes, say, "Hmm"
I'll make notes, ask which is "Good…or better?"

Of your history file, I have no need
You've heard it read aloud tonight
Be assured, this exam will not take long
The prescription scribbled in a flash

Please seat yourself upon this chair
The crucial test will now begin
Hold your chin upon your thumb
Look forward; tell me what you see

Round faces? Are you sure that's all?
Look left are they smiling now?

Is that <u>good</u>; or look right; <u>better</u>? Keep the chin
firm on the thumb Now close your eyes
and press Your hands upon your head Can you see future sights
Spinning 'round your brain? *Breakfast dishes left*
by Sally Going out the door? <u>Good</u>?
(Eyes closed, chin up) Now washing Garden
tools perhaps? Better? Press harder and
breathe deeply now

Sweeter scenes are coming into view Flower
shapes of orchid hue? <u>Good</u>?
Volunteer Chair of flower show-- <u>Better</u>? Eyes
open please, hands in lap I'll use my light
check closer... Hmmm.
I see foreign words in far-off land. <u>good</u>? Sally's
there to hold your hand; <u>better</u>?

A wide collage fills those futuring spaces
Golf clubs fishing poles turn into an artist's brush
Clarinet noise mingle 'round; <u>good</u>?
Car is parked; back pain gone; <u>better</u>?

My appointment schedule's full tonight
Must cut this short; I'm sure you understand'
Overall retirement perspectives are fine;
Senior living won't require drastic changes

Please note I've written on the pad:
"This prescription will take time to fill"
The lens must be ground with love;
And reflect life in thoughtful ways

Please fit 'to happy Chin-Up frames
Provide cleaning cloth which will
Turn tear-stains into fun spots
Enclose in case marked "Better."

Written for Shelly by "mums" Esther (paper
artistry by Pete) for his Retirement Party,
June 26, 1999

Reflections on Adult Adoptions

She was puzzled, "I think I *misunderstood*; you said
you are *adopting* Sally?"
I grinned, "No, you have it right. It's a treasured decision."
"But why?" she asked, "Don't you already have four?"
"Well, yes," I answered, "but Ben has two and I have two;
We want on *together*!!"
She was thoughtful – spared mentioning our ages…
"Besides," I continued, "Pennie's never had a sister."
"What are you going to name this new little girl?"
She coyly queried.
"The 5th Child," was my response.
"I've heard it all!" She took her head.

Still groping for words, she began again,
She is a Teacher/Librarian and married; am I correct?"
I nodded in assent and smiled!
"We're counting on them for our first grandchild!"
"Don't rush this process," she came back fast;
"How do you know their marriage is going to last?
Plus that husband hasn't been given a name!!"
"Their Union will last; somehow we know!!
His name…hmmm this may sound wild, maybe he'll
end up being the 6th Child"
"Perfect material," she countered with a grin,
"For Ben's next lecture on 'Zero Population."

Thirty-eight years have gone by since my friend and I conversed.
Thirty-eight years! How fast they have flown!
Highlights would take another page, but one stands out.
Our long wait in Kaiser had just begun,
It was the 5th Child who held the family together as one!

**CHEERS, 5th AND 6th
ON THE BIG 40!!**

Relativity Retired?

The Rumor is that Howard has
Retired
No, no, these are just State
Employee words
Beyond Golf, he'll practice his
Profession!
An Architect's Brain, you see
Is made in a Special Way
It keeps going night and day
Sleep brings a bit of Slowing
Down... then
ZOOM! He wakes with a Different
Plan!
It's just the way a Creative
person's made!
Oh they also travel, but they
Study
On the way
So Creativity's NEVER RETIRED.
I say!

Remembering Almanor

John was on time at the Train Station
GOOD OMEN for Start of the CELEBRATION
On North by Fields of Rice and many Trees
Fruits & Nuts; are there any Bees?
Past the Golf Course; up the Hill
Take the Third Stop which says Oroville
They are there to meet us the couple sweet
Chris and Larry – all ready to eat!
Good Conversation - - - All of us lots to say
But before we know it, we're on our way!
Next town is Chico - not very far
Specially in this Red Rental Car!
Up the Hill now to Forest Ranch
We barely stop to give it a Glance
The sign says: PLUMAS State PaDoes that mean "Safe
in DaSmooth Paving; Engineer Praise Still, did he have to
leave so many curves? At last arrive in the town of Chester not
everything is familiar to Estat Forward east – driving near Lake
Almanor

Yes, we've been in this place before!
Up the Hill, get ready to turn right
Everywhere trees are a lovely sight.
We are stopping at the OFFICIAL Gate
It's to the RENTAL HOUSE we now relate
ego-theOn w Franklin

Rhododendrons For Natalie

Trying, trying to understand
Then Pennie's words brought change
Half a smile joined with
A bit of nodding, blinking

Natalie was trying too
With teen-age talk
Waiting for Swiss response
Now blue lights began to shine
Brows went up, happy lips opened

Words still stuck in pretty throat
Pushing, pushing to come out
Larry tried a bit of Schweitzer Deutch
(He'd stumbled on the language path)
Water fun brought little laughs
Wide, wide eyes spoke volumes

Wurst was the wondrous word
Which brought forth, "Yes!"
"I Like it very much," came next
Eager eyes emphasized full well
Food she had been missing

Can this be Miss Fritze
Chatting now with Howard?
Conversation goes back and forth
Excited eyes are speaking too
Winks say she gets D's joke

Scenic sites and swimming meets
Roller coaster through her brain
Or is it Music she'll remember?
What will I recall?
Lilian with the Laughing Eyes

RHODODENDRONS FOR NATALIE

Can it be? The day has arrived!
Blossoms are bright pink on the bush.

Sally: Treasured Teacher

Accept bouquets skilled special friend
You've made reading come alive
We've cheered your gentle guidance
The patient paths you chose

Many students now still young
Will look back in fifty years
Thank their luck or heaven
For the gift that they were given

As you leave now, move on
Finding magic in new ways
Don't forget us oldies here
Who'll remember you with praise

Silver Pieces In The Sunset

Silver Pieces in the Sunset – A Gift to you all
Forgive the Old Lady is she lets a Tear Fall

Don't you YOUNG ONES dare start Grieving
About the gifts you are Receiving

Instead, time now, to start JOYFUL CHATTER
How you will USE your bowl or your PLATTER

TIME, of course, to Indulge in FOND MEMORIES
Of how they were used by FRANKLIN families

NEW YEARS DAY Heads the Fun Group!
YOU Start Serving SPECIAL OYSTER SOUP

So now let's all begin to SMILE and SING

SILVER PIECES IN THE SUNSET

Hugs and Love

Sugar Bowl Memories

We had gone to the Carl's home for dinner
(That was Aunt Beth and Uncle Forest)
I was intrigued with their dish which held sugar.
Though only four years old, I gave myself a Goal..
Someday, I would own a lovely Sugar Bowl.
Flowers painted on it would be light blue and green
Yet every tiny artistic detail could be seen.

     I turned six, started to the one-room Sunrise School
It was close-by; my brother and I did not need the bus
One teacher taught all eight grades, including Art
I knew Miss Myers must be very, very smart!

     The Dust Storms came; the Carls moved away
Forest to the CCC; Beth & Paul to Salt Lake to stay
Then Mother, my brother, and I were on the bus
Turns out, the Buskirks are taking in all of us.

     I'm at Stewart School, East High, and U of U
The Felkners now live in a in a Home with view
The Carls haven't purchased; they still Rent
We climb Stairs to reach their Apartment
When I visit, guess what I tell Aunt Beth once more?
You're right; "It's your lovely Sugar Bowl I adore!"

     The shock or War makes all of us grieve
My brother my cousins, my friends all leave.
The Navy Lieutenant comes into my life…
Before long, I agree to be his wife.
The Wedding is large, Sorority Sisters Sing
What is the Gift that Aunt Beth will bring?

     "How old is it? I ask through tears?
"I'm not sure, but Quite a few Years!"

So today, Derek and Val, I'm passing it to you
You know it is coming with much love too!
My Math isn't great, I've often been told,

<u>I think</u>, in 2019, it will be 100 Year old!!

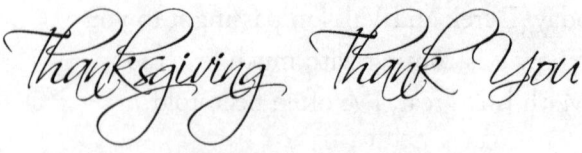

Thanksgiving Thank You

Every single one of us here today
Can say THANKS in his or her own way
ALL of us are mixing the Get Together Glad
With an Extra Special Kind of Sad
I ask you now to Open Wide Your Eyes
Do the Taylors Show a LOOK OF SURPRISE?
MY THANK – YOU in Front of all of You
Is to Pennie & Howard for All They Do!!
After My FALL, I MUST CONFESS
I Was a Special Kind of MESS
Your Patience, Your Care – Endless Hours!
Please Accept TONS OF THANKFUL Flowers!

Written by MUMS for the Taylors, Thanksgiving 2019

Welcome to the Family!!

Listen carefully now TRISH DEAR
To A word we 'specially want you to HEAR
You probably have heard it before
It may help to hear it once more
On that SPECIAL NOVEMBER NINETEEN
YOU will be the FAMILY QUEEN!
It'll be UNIQUE for the FAMILY Too
That's why we're PUSHING it to YOU
As you may have had a HUNCH
We're a Many Backgrounds Bunch
But ALL Of US want you to know
There's ONE QUALITY we'd like to SHow
Each of us now EXTENDS A HAND
PLEASE, PLEASE, UNDERSTAND

YOU'RE WELCOME!!!!

FAMILY BIRTHDAYS

Can It Be

Can this be the precious baby from whom we all
waited?
That baby who wanted no relative to hold her –
excepting her mother>

Can this be the toddler who played in the Almanor
Snow
- even though it was Easter?

Can this be the angel who danced in the Nutcracker
and planned a career in Ballet?

Then she was THE SUPER SWIMMER --
the Medal-Winning Champ

On the Captain of the Water Polo Team
at McClatchy High

Could that have been our Natalie-one of a Trio
Singing to the High School Graduation Crowd?

Her next focus was on Turtles down in Costa Rica --
Environmental Reasons, of course!

What did we miss while she concentrated so hard?
on Studies, while home was the Dorm?

Time races; the University is in Spain,
but Travelling too is part of the plan:

Holidays with Relatives in the Alps to snowboard,
then Easter with the Pope, plus Venice too

How many countries? Were there really ten?
And how did the African markets fit it?

Home to Chaos re financing the State U System
Another year? Plus tuition going up?
Not 5 years! Change; the Major to Spanish and
Work unbelievably hard!!

Can it be? She did it, and now
She's GRADUATE NATALIE with her B.A!

We all are very PROUD of you,
Miss GLOBAL CITIZEN

Still, truthfully, (maybe wistfully)
Nana asks, "CAN IT BE?"

From Nana --, Natalie's graduation from
         San Francisco State University,
         May 21, 2011

Discovery 21

Columbus sailed forth, so we've been told
To prove the world was round
Was he quiet amazed at what he found?

Cervantes used his wit to bring two men to life
Or was it really just his pen
Creating all that strife?

Founding Fathers then forged on
Declaring they must war – push evil rulers
From this stolen shore

Discovery now moved down a very different path
Machines were quickly being built
To cut man's work in half

Women pushed beyond the suffrage pace
On TV we saw droves of them
Leading in the race
Doctors rivaled Doctors in search of human genes
Allied with the corporate gang and
The word is SPEED – the Moon's a blast
Musicians found they too
Must write and rocket fast

So *Drummer Youth*, as all of this you scan
What is it that you seek
To prove yourself a man?

Use those twenty sticks and one
To beat a better drum

Discover a *new path to peace*
<u>Invite your friends to come!</u>

Memories

Memories are special – very Special
They can make us fell Joy
They can make us feel Pain
A Memory can make you feel Old
A Memory can make you feel Young
I, Esther Franklin, think Middle-Age
Memories
Are the very best of all the rest!
So, dear Cleo, as you face this
Painful Current Challenge
Recall when you were FIRSTLADY
Of the SCIENCE KING HANK as you
Took off on your first "Different"
TRAVEL ADVENTURE"

Written especially for Cleo-Kocol
By Esther Franklin-July 3, 2016

Natalie – Turning 30

October 16; what will I say??
To Natalie on this SPECIAL DAY??
There was the Baby who could scream ALARMS
Unless she was held in MOTHER'S ARMS
How did she "move on" to Ten-year-old? Now guess!
You're right – the one who was in Spanish Dress
Your first Medal was real, real Cool!
For SWIMMING GREAT at McKinley POOL
The reason it was especially GREAT
You were so YOUNG – JUST EIGHT!
ON to High School; then at what age?
Were you up Singing on the Stage??
When did Nana move on too, do you suppose?
Was it when she started writing PROSE?
"Neologistic" Is that a word?
Probably one you'd never heard!
Monthly Newsletters you now received
When they stopped; were you relieved?
You hadn't been to Spain just yet
The Exact year I now forget
Was it in Madrid that we met you?
Or did you come to Barcelona too?
Other Euro Countries you visited a Plenty
I think maybe it was Twenty!
Swiss Relatives were on the Christmas Slate
To "Au Tanenbaum" did you Relate?
That Summer Cousin Lillian was the Bravo
Who came to visit us in Sacto
Back in California at CSUSan Fran
Believe the NEW NEWS if you can!
FIVE YEARS, NOT FOUR You're Told

Then you Take a Step SO BOLD!!
Problems with KINESEOLOGY will VANISH
IF You just CHANGE your MAJOR to Spanish!
You HANG IN and Before too Long
We're down to sing the Graduation Song
MOVING, TRAVELLING; A BUSY KID!
Can't Believe All the Things You Did!
CITED For EXCELLENCE with your St Mary's MA
SWIM COACH or PROFESSOR; Which do We Say?
I'm 'searching for words
Now Escaping like Birds
Except Natalie, GRAND KID, I PLEDGE TO YOU
I'LL LOVE YOU – <u>No Matter What you Do!!</u>

Written by Nana for Natalie, October 16, 2019

Nathaniel Turning 40

In San Diego, the NEWS came by phone
Sally and Shelley – no longer alone
Their voices really buzzed with JOY!
Yes, their Special BABY was a BOY!
"PA BEN" knew it had barely begun
This Kid was gonna be a lot of Fun!
Science was really not Ben's Field
<u>Not</u> to the ZOO; we'd have to Yield
PA didn't take Nate to see Alligators
No, he took him to Observe LEGISLATORS!
Pa was Major Entertainer; we all knew
There was your COUSIN DEREK too.
Or was N K THE ONE to KNOW??
WHERE in WATER Feet should go?
Both Boys began to grow with Speed
<u>Lots of folks</u> they had to Heed
At FIVE came the BIGGEST BLOW!
Down the "DIABETUS" Road you'd Go
"No SUGAR" all of us began to say –
THAT has lasted for NANA 'til Today
At School; why did you Pass OUT?
Nana rushed to see what it was About
The Ambulance had already arrived
At Kaiser I learned you had Survived!
Times and Schools pass on too fast
Arden, Rio, and Los Rios at last
But, the Biggest Word by Far
Starts with "C" --- I <u>do mean</u> CAR!!
Another one now takes its Place
It is accompanied by a Pretty Face
You know this one is a very Special Dish!!

Of course I mean the Unique "TRISH"
We Hear coming sometime in November
Is a Day WE will ALL REMEMBER
The most IMPORTANT DAY of Your Life
The DAY You Call Trish <u>"WIFE"</u>!!

Written by NANA for NATE for his 40th Birthday
October 13,2019

Teen Time

TEA TIME brought out our best
What will TEEN TIME do?
No doubt TEAM will be a major word

All these T's which take us Back and
Forth in time.

Memory brings the creeping climber
On the stairs; gazing back with
Triumphant look of Della 2

Then travel times – to Beach, next Almanor
The climb was then the hill of snow
Triumphant still, and face aglow

Virginia coast, the Atlantic blue
Did that appeal to you? Perhaps, but...
Recall talks of indoor pool

Our dancing doll; how many shows?
The angel holding harp so firm
Many roles, but always face of joy

Holidays were urgent times
Why waste endless hours on food,
When there were ribbons yet to cut?

You begged from other on "All Hallows Day"
Yet you gave more when you appeared
In Spanish dancer's dress!

From tiny, sturdy swimmer at the "Y"
You grew and swam and swam and grew
'Til medals tell of Time in different ways

To future times we now must gaze
Put out your gifted palms
What does the future read?

Pools and pools of blue we see
Fun, work, and friends – all three
Possibly some shining trophies too

A hundred books you'll read, for sure
Then writing is your next allure
How many boys will you endure?

Ballet-Tap might be your next artistic try
Or singer-actress may be your thing
"Starring Natalie" we'll buy, we'll buy!

Scientist, Therapist, your flag's unfurled
Or just Ambassador to save the world
Dreams are all around you curled

Keep uncles, aunts and cousins near
Close family to allay your fears
All join now to say "TEEN TIME CHEERS"

For Natalie from Nana
On your 13th birthday

Turning Eighteen

Now you're eighteen
Whee, you can vote!
And Nana is urging
"Go for Gravel!"
Plus "Call your Senatore"
"Vote to Withdraw!"

You already know about
"Studies Come First!"
Whatever happened to??
"Go for FUN!"??

Now you're <u>mature</u>
(Or at lest, almost)
You're understanding more
How history relates to present day

You're also entering the time
Of making good choices
That information isn't all in books
Nor in professor's heads
It takes practice and learning to feel
We all are learning each day

My hope, my darling,
Is that as you choose
You'll find life's riches
In weighing the concerns
And needs of others

Happy birthday and much love
For Natalie from Nana-October 16, 2007

Turning Seventy-Five

I met you first as a Dr.
We visited your mother in those days
Then you became a Student
Of Business at Sacramento State
Your new M.A. put you on the Road
Back and Forth to Berkeley you went
You were a Kaiser Executive now!
Telling other Eye Doctors how to Offer Service
YOU Went on a TRIP with SON NATE!
When did you become a SIXTH SON of mine?
Did we honor you when you RETIRED?
Can it be you became another Student?
You are MSTER GARDENER now!
(Curiosity pushes me,)
Do you love your wife as much as
YOU love ORCHIDS?
Orchid take you Overseas!
Are you Slowing Down?
What NEW ROLE
Are you going to play?
Whatever it is,
WE KNOW YOU WILL PAY IT WELL!

HAPPY BIRTHDAY and LOVE
Mums Esther November 16, 20168

For FRIENDS
BEYOND FAMILY

Birgitta, Turning 89

Campus Commons Residence
Has been Our Meeting Place
We are now CLOSE FRIENDS
How did it happen, DEAR ONE?
Your Current Memory Falters
But MEMORIE OF SWEDEN
EUROPE too are quite clear
I think you help me remember
My trip to Sweden with PETE
(Did we really stay in a HOSTEL
On the River in STOCKHOLM?)
ENJOY Today; and WE will Plan
To Continue our GOOD FRIENDSHIP

By Esther Franklin, January 25, 2020

Celebrating Seventy!!

Can it be? Is Pat REALLY turning seven-zero?
Memories are special--- VERY SPECIAL
They can make us feel Joy
But they also can make us feel Pain
I remember meeting the <u>Pratts at UU</u>
My husband said that <u>he</u> had agreed
To take care of the Pratt children
If there was an "Emergency" in another
Country in which the "Pratt Team"
Was donating Special Medical Care
Did Pat know about the <u>"Husband's Deal"</u>?
Next there was the FLOOD of 1982
All the Pratts took Refuge in OUR STUDIO

<u>My invitation</u> read: "Peace Mission to Libya"
I replied I'd go if Pat Pratt could come too.
Your focus was Medical Care; mine Education
Did we really do all those "Presentations"?
More countries, continents and OPERATIONS
Now living in the Capital of New Zealand
Had Fred REALLY walked the whole country
On a very, very SPECIAL PEACE MARCH?
When home, you CHAIRED UU Art Committee
Arranging many SHOWS, including Pete's.
2006 brought bad news of Fred's illness
Still he Persisted with Wondrous Strength
FINALLY we had to say Goodbye. I knew the
FEELINGS. I'd known the GRIEF 6 YEARS BEFORE
2009-OUR TURN in India with YOUR PRECISE ADVICE
DOCTORATES for 2 daughters; I shared your PRIDE!
Enjoyed the LOVELY WEDDINGS too.

2015 I went to the Hague; and then I was 90!
Pennie made the big plans for FUN at Tahoe
Who was my ROOMMATE to be? Pat, of course
SO MANY MEMORIES – SO MUCH LOVE!!
*WE ALL SALUTE YOU, DEAR ONE **TURNING SEVENTY***
For Patricia Pratt from Esther Franklin

Inga Turning 60

How did it Begin to Be?
There was A girl who was at Rio High
Then she did to Stanford fly
U GRADUATE she was in old Vienna
And what do you think came next?
She spoke German without a Text!
Talking to Germans is a lot of FUN
From Old Folks down to a Little One
Maybe a Course or Two at STATE?
But Travel & Fun were on the Slate
Oh Inga, Dear One, Shall we CHEER
How many Men have called you "Dear"?
For all those numbers that we POST
We Raise our Glasses High in TOAST
"RETURNING to SACTO" is the WORD
Are you sure I'm not Absurd?
Soon We'll be Saluting You Again
After that, I'll Say "AMEN"!
Then, <u>for Sure</u>, Our Gentle Warrior
PROMISE US, You Will Become a LAWYER!

Lilian

Lilian speaks with her eyes

At first we saw bashful eyes
Trying, trying to understand
Then Pennie's words brought change
Half a smile joined with
A bit of nodding, blinking

Natalie was trying too
With teen-age talk
Waiting for Swiss response
Now blue lights began to shine
Brows went up, happy lips opened

Words still stuck in pretty throat
Pushing, pushing to come out
Larry tried a bit of Schweitzer Deutch
(He'd stumbled on the language path)
Water fun brought little laughs
Wide, wide eyes spoke volumes

Wurst was the wondrous word
Which brought forth, "Yes!"
"I Like it very much," came next
Eager eyes emphasized full well
Food she had been missing

Can this be Miss Fritze
Chatting now with Howard?
Conversation goes back and forth
Excited eyes are speaking too
Winks say she gets D's joke

Scenic sites and swimming meets
Roller coaster through her brain
Or is it Music she'll remember?
What will I recall?
Lillian with the Laughing Eyes

Senior Teenager

I
JUST discovered your age group! You
Are a Seenager (Senior) teenager. You
Have everything you wanted as a teenager,
Only 55-65 year later, you
Don't have to go to school, or work. you
get an allowance every month. You have
your own pad. You don't have a curfew. You
have a driver's license and you own your
own car. You have ID that gets you into bars
and the Wine Store. People you hang out
with are not afraid of getting pregnant. They
aren't scared of anything. They have been
blessed to live this long, so why be scared?
And you don't have acne. Life is <u>Good!</u> Also,
YOU will feel much more intelligent after
reading this, if YOU are a SEENAGER. Brains
of older people are slow because they know
so much. If you go to another room and
Wonder why you came, it's not a Problem,
It's Nature's
Way of making older people get
Exercise. SO THERE!

HUGS TO DAVID JACOBS, AUGUST 28, 2018

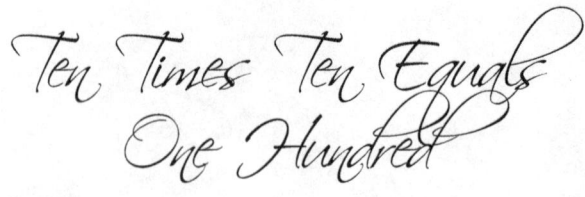

Ten Times Ten Equals One Hundred

An earlier Poet said, "Let us count the Ways"
We can sing Mary Harris Praise
One Hundred there are, of course
But space does not allow on this one page
So, for now, we will list TEN
At a later date, we'll begin again.
NUMBER ONE: starts her Study Journey at what is now
Cal State U San Fran
NUMBER TWO: Graduate Studies earn her two MA's
She's deserving of much Praise!
NUMBER THREE: Foreign Classes include Paris
NUMBER FOUR: ART Classes the "Creative" Harris
NUMBER FIVE: Teaching now – Many Hours!
(Elementary Students bring her Flowers)
NUMBER SIX: Political Mary emerges now
NUMBER SEVEN: Now P.R. Institute to W.F.A.
NUMBER EIGHT: SECRETARY of D World Feds
NUMBER NINE: Keeps CLIMBING 160STEPS
NUMBER TEN: CELEBRATES! AN ART SHOW!!
WE MADE T TO TEN, BUT THERE'S
SO MUCH MORE WE COULD SAY ABOUT
THIS MARY WE ALL ADORE!
For MARY WITH LOVE from Esther
June 25, 2017

Un-Loved Hearts

"Does House-Sharing Work?"
My Cousin said to me
She Smiled, Eyes Down
"It's not my...I mean...
Do you......... are you...?"
Yes....; no...... I said.
Widows don't choose,
I went on...................
But one can't love
Conveniences; can one?...
I tried; I yearned for love again
They come...... the house
Turns into home
"Do you cry?"
No; His Music Helps
Widows must feel only Gratitude
Their Tears are only Dry
Their Un-loved Hearss
DON'T DANCE

"Uncelebrated Birthday"

Some folks turning Seventy-Five
Would say they were glad
Just to be alive!
They would accept – not condemn
All the goodies given them
Then there's this person who –
(Is really, really friendly too--)
Whisper her name if you can
Softly now, "It's Diane."
Her husband's name is Jim
We can SHOUT kudo's about him!
Their Home is full of Memories
How many people know of these?
The Dining Table was Extra Long
Also the place for many a Song
In Early Years, Little Kids were there
They've "grown up" with Homes to Share
Is Esther Courageous to stand up here
Reviewing Memories you don't want to hear?
She hopes they won't make you SAD
That ALL of us can be REAL GLAD
At This VERY, VERY UNUSUAL
"UNCELEBRATED BIRTHDAY" LUNCH

AFTER DEATHS

Robertsons: Treasured Friends

Accept bouquets Skilled Special Friends
You've made United Nations come alive
We've cheered your gentle guidance
The creative paths you chose
Many members can recall the Chair
Willing to take on duo roles
How long Editor, Duane?
An Eternity or So
Behind this Marvel Man, we knew
Of course, ...the woman...
Izzy, it was you!
So sweet in greeting, every meeting!
Future members will look back
Hear the Legend of the Team
Thank their luck or heaven
For the gift that all were given

They Called Him "Doc"

They're not here to share fond thoughts
To marvel at his deeds
To read the many plaques of praise
See twisted faces turned to smiles

Nor do they know that messages of loss
Arrive from 'round the globe
World Federalist, Amnesty International--
Words in languages they don't speak

They just knew the Clinic man
Who helped them when they hurt
The guy who laughed and hugged them
The one whom they called "Doc"

They're not here, for they've no clothes
One wears to honor greatness
Nor do they have the cars of gas
Or directions to this place

Yet if we use our hearts to see
We find that they surround this room
Remind us: use the skills you have
Help some person every day

Precinct walk, sweep up the floor
Change the world in your own way
Make choices you've not made before
Then "Doc" has helped us all

Written with love for Pat and
family by Esther Franklin with
fond remembrances of happy
times we shared with Fred

Written with love for Pat and
family by Esther Franklin with
fond remembrances of happy
times we shared with Fred

UNIQUE

Beggar Boy

I cannot take your PHOTO, BEGGAR BOY

NO; POLISH CODE Forbids It
DECENCY is the LAW

Yet I carry a PICTURE of YOU
Along in My Mind

Black Curls Rim the
Dirty Brown Face

Broad SHOELESS FEET

Those SAD EYES Raised Up
With Your Hands to BEG

WHY YOU, BEGGAR BOY???
WHY NOT MY GRANDSON??

Quiet Inspiration

ESR's Tribute to Robert Smith

(Recipient: "Faculty Member of the Year"
Sierra College; August 1993)

We've read words, know men
Who live lives
Of Quiet Desperation

Hear now of one
Who'd lived and lives
A life of Quiet Inspiration

The meeting was boring
Plans had to be made
He was there

The envelopes were endless
Mailings had to go out
He was there

Conference room chairs
Had to be moved
He was there

Ten of tables
Had to be staffed
He was there

Multiple causes which
Needed his help
He was there

One more answer for
Students who ask
He was there

A crowd must convene
On the Capitol steps
He was there

In August's heat
The march must go on
He was there

In December's cold
Vigil lights must shine
He was there

One more person
Whose hurt needed healing
He was there

Not the Podium One
Who speaks with
Leader's loud lips

He's the STEADY ONE
Who silently serves
He's always there

Thank you, Bob for all you do

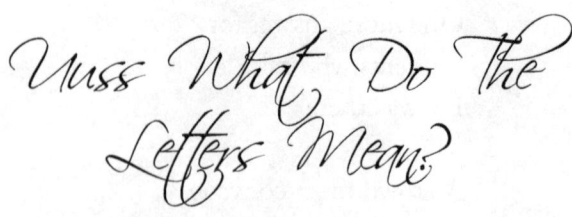

UUSS What Do The Letters Mean?

Friends say, "To which Church do you go?"
Is your answer often pretty slow?
The UUSS, as it Now turns out
Has HISTORY we can all Muse about
The 70's found TED WEBB as PREACHER
Then SOCIEL ACTION was his FEATURE
FORUMS were held at Half Past Nine
Well-Known Speakers Suited All Just Fine
Ted RETIRED; the Scene began to Change
Emphasis had quite a Broad New Range
Some Members said, "Now call us CHUCH!"
3 Votes Left those people in the LURCH
OFFICIALLY it is Current Propriety
Say, "Unitarian Universalist SOCIETY"
FOCUS too Shifts as Time Goes By
"They're so SPIRITUAL" some people Sigh
Tuesday Mornings – HERE'S THE SCOOP!
JOIN the TED WEBB DISCUSSION GROUP

Written by Esther Franklin – December 10, 2019

Youth in Western Jeans

Our Eyes Touch
Each Others Eyes
Your Hands Press My Hands
A gleaming Axis
Gyrates Your Globe

What's Agrarian Nice to You?
Who knows or Persons
Born to Toil

And Lovers Too and Lovers
Enough of Status
Dictating Down
Across a World, Your
Comrads Walk
In Tight Designer Jeans

Your Plastic Plans
Provide New Thrills
Beyond Dull
Basic Bread
Whose Dreams
Are Real?

These Women Like
Your Loving Looks
They've known Youth
And Lovers too
They are not here
To Preach

They know of Eyes and Touch

Like You, their History Gone

Walk and Rally, Say Brave Words
Of Work for 5-Year Plans
Like LEARNING TO READ

Do you know of WORK and CAUSE?

Written in a Park in Sofia, Bulgaria

List of Poems

CPSIA information can be obtained
at www.ICGtesting.com
Printed in the USA
BVHW071021270220
573527BV00001B/106